EXTREME

Calendar
Circle Time
By: Deb Wagner

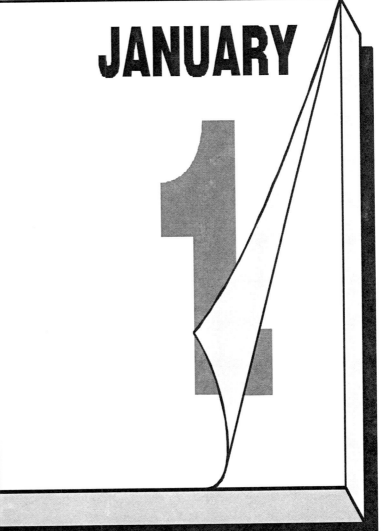

JANUARY

1

Crown Wagner Publishing

Book and cover design: Deborah Wagner

ISBN13: 978-0-9834805-0-1

To My Husband, Doug

My Best Friend

First, I would like to thank God for being with me every step of the way during the process of this book. Secondly, I would like to acknowledge, my husband, Doug, who spent countless hours on the computer to make this dream a reality. And last, but certainly not least, I would like to thank my co-workers, church family, and my friends and family who encouraged me to do this. Thank you everyone...I am so blessed!

Deb Wagner

Table of Contents

Foreword

After 45 years as an educator in Special Education, I have developed a keen eye and deep appreciation for programs that actually promote student success. Education is such a 'serious place' now-a-days and so many children have become anxious and fearful about learning. Learning programs that meld the idea of having fun AND learning important material is extremely difficult to come across!

On many occasions I have observed Deb Wagner work with a group of students for 'Calendar time'. These students do NOT sit still and they typically have the attentive time span of ten to fifteen minutes. These students are competitive and social inept. Sharing, giving compliments and encouraging their classmates are competencies we work on for years. These students do not test well and the results from standardized testing is often disappointing.

During <u>Extreme Calendar Time</u> these same students are paying special attention and often are engaged for over one hour! These same students are encouraging each other and they are learning the power of 'group thinking'. We track student performance on the yearly testing and these students show increased scores/percentiles in knowledge and participation.

You can't argue with success! <u>Extreme Calendar Time</u> is a rare program that is inclusive, innovative, enjoyable and does support student learning. I highly recommend this program's use in every type and age of elementary school students.

Ellen S. Server, Ed.S.

Great Asset for the Special Education Classroom! This edition has proven to be an excellent tool to address AKS goals in a structured and fun way for my special education students. It keeps the students actively engaged in learning. The kids really enjoy all the activities and look forward to participating in Calendar every day.

Leslie Bruce
29 year veteran special education teacher

Extreme Calendar is a student focused approach to engaging calendar activities on a wide variety of academic/grade level topics. The 'Calendar Queen' has provided activities, as well as websites available for building your own Extreme Calendar time. This approach to a daily calendar segment supports vocabulary across subject areas, as well as test taking strategies. Students are encouraged to think through why answers are correct or incorrect and also presents multiple choice strategies. Extreme Calendar offers practice in basic skills (which many students are lacking), but also higher order thinking skills like analogies. Always included in Extreme Calendar are activities on manners, values and problem solving scenarios. Students experience successful outcomes throughout calendar time.

Michele Matol-Ferguson, Ed.S.
Coordinator
Oakland Meadow School

Extreme Calendar provides a fun, lively and engaging approach to calendar time. Not only are there many great examples of actual activities but there are ideas provided which will help you in the development of your own activities. The author has vast experience in working with students with learning difficulties and this book offers daily opportunities for increasing skills in higher order thinking, social skills and a variety of basic academics.

David Ashton
Principal
Oakland Meadow School

Introduction

I have put together what I think is a great plan to introduce Calendar every day. I work with EBD (Emotional Behavior Disorder) students in Gwinnett County, Georgia and have found that they need a Calendar that keeps them engaged and cover a wide spectrum of knowledge outside the typical Calendar time.

I have created Calendar using a "playing game" approach. We choose a different student to be the Calendar helper every day. They get to choose the sequence of topics and even choose the question in the topic container. They are rewarded with 'classroom bucks' (play money) which they save and spend on Friday during our "Trading Post" time. Many of the topics I use a few months a year to give the students a variety and to keep the Calendar fresh. Many of the topics are seasonal and holiday appropriate.

The reaction of the students appears positive and they feel successful after each Calendar session.

I hope you find this information very useful.

Chapter 1
On This Day

I use any unique holidays that I can find on the internet for each day. A good resource is www.teachervision.com. Teachervision.com has the 'Educator's Calendar' and www.enchantedlearning.com has a 'Monthly Activity Calendar'.

In this section, I introduce some important events that happened on this day in history.

Some examples of this might be...

March 2, 1904 Dr. Seuss's birthday.

March 3, 1847 Alexander Graham Bell's birthday

March 4, 1979 Voyager I discovered that Jupiter has rings

March 5, 1868 Stapler was invented

I also announce a nonsense event. Many of these I find on www.brownielocks.com which lists very unusual celebrations for each day.

Some examples of this might be...

April 14 International Moment of Laughter Day - To celebrate this day, simply tell jokes or do funny things that cause people to laugh.

April 15 Titanic Remembrance Day - Remembrance Day is dedicated to the memory of the Titanic, and over 1500 people who died.

April 16 National Librarian Day - Celebrate the day by sending a card to your librarian. Visit the library today, and make certain to say hello and "Thank you" to all of the librarians.

Chapter 2
Poetry

This is one section that I only use a few months a year. I begin with Nursery Rhymes, introducing a new Nursery Rhyme every day. I find that many elementary school age children currently have never learned their nursery rhymes. We read the rhyme and explore the history. Many of these rhymes I found on www.rhymes.org.uk. An example might be "Little Miss Muffet". Little Miss Muffet was a small girl whose name was Patience Muffet. Her stepfather, Dr. Muffet wrote the first scientific catalog of British insects. While eating her breakfast of curds and whey, Little Miss Muffet was frightened by one of the spiders and ran away! After this, I introduce a silly poem using the same rhyme.

An example of this is...

Little Miss Muffet sat on a tuffet

Eating a Big Mac and Fries

Along came a spider and sat down beside her

'Yuck', it said, 'I prefer flies'.

Usually the last of the year, I find gross, rude and funny poems for the students to enjoy. Kenn Nesbitt, Bruce Lansky, Eric Ode, Neal Levin, and Trevor Harvey are some of my favorite authors. Samples of their work can be found on the internet. An example of Kenn Nesbitt's "The Tighty-Whity Spider" found on www.Poetry4Kids.com is as follows.

The Tighty Whity Spider went down the waterslide

Got a water wedgie halfway down the ride

Jumped up and screamed and ran around in pain

Now the Tighty-Whity spider will not do that again.

Chapter 3
U.S.A. Trivia

I use this section all year. It helps promote map reading, presidents, capitals, mountain ranges, rivers and lakes and especially history. I bought the U.S.A. Trivia game but there are many websites on the internet with multiple choice trivia questions. A good website for this might be www.jimloy.com. Once there, scroll down and select 'Puzzles', scroll down to the 'Trivia' entry and select 'USA States Trivia'. An additional website is www.funtrivia.com.

Examples I use are:

Which city is known as the "City of Brotherly Love"?

A. Philadelphia, B. Atlanta C. Houston

Name a Great Lake that borders the state of Michigan.

A. Lake Ontario B. Lake Superior

Which mountain system extends from Maine to Alabama?

A. Appalachian B. Rocky

Name the capital of Kansas?

A. Kansas City B. Topeka C. Wichita

If the student gets the answer right, they are rewarded with play money which they can spend on Friday at the Trading Post. If the student is not sure of the answer, they can choose to call on another student for help, and then, they have to split the money.

Chapter 4
Science Trivia

In my quest to touch upon a little of every academic subject during Calendar, science is one of their favorites. I either incorporate the science section that we are covering in class or find areas that they are really interested in with the hopes of peaking their interest so they research the subject later on their own. I try to find questions that are multiple choice or true and false to help them build their confidence in answering and decide which answer makes the most sense. This also gives us a chance to decide why the other answers are incorrect.

A good website for this is www.sciencespot.net.

An example of this is...

Which of the following scientists studies animals?

A. Botanist   B. Zoologist   C. Geologist

Which is hotter?

A. 100 degrees Fahrenheit   B. 100 degrees Celsius

Which is lighter?

A. Cold air   B. Hot air

Which planet is known for its rings?

A. Mars   B. Jupiter   C. Saturn

Chapter 5

Three Sentence Game

This activity helps students develop their thoughts to compose a paragraph. We play this everyday and each student is given a different writing prompt. They verbally create a topic sentence, a supporting sentence and a concluding sentence and I use those terms to remind them of the major parts of a paragraph. There are many sources for writing prompts but one of my favorites is www.canteach.ca. Once there, select the 'English Language Arts' entry under the 'Elementary Resources' section, then select 'Writing Prompts & Journal Topics'.

An example might be:

1. What would it be like to hike through a forest?

2. How could you change your bedroom if you could decorate it any way.

3. Describe how we can save energy?

4. What might you be saving your birthday money for?

5. What makes you feel safe?

6. When are you the happiest?

Chapter 6

Sign Language

Sign Language is such a beautiful language and the students enjoy learning it. We had a hearing impaired student that they enjoyed knowing what she was saying. There are many books at the library and websites to get the signing from. A website that I use is www.teach-nology.com. Select the 'Printables' tab then select the 'Sign Language Flashcards' entry on the left hand side. Here are some examples...

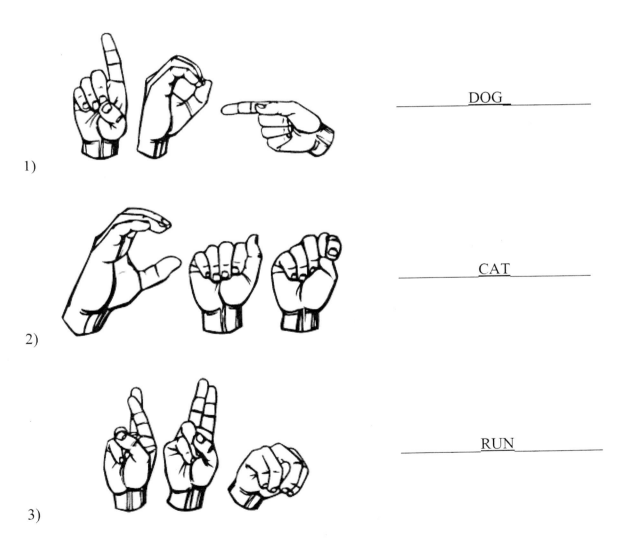

1)   _____DOG_____

2)   _____CAT_____

3)   _____RUN_____

Chapter 7
Analogies

We practice analogies every day because they are another component of the CRCT. We used word analogies and math analogies so the student never knows what they are picking out of the bag to do that day. Some seasonal analogies are on www.enchantedlearning.com and I also use www.rhlschool.com. Once there, select 'English Grammar and Usage' then select 'Analogies'.

A simple analogy would be...

Friend is to pal as fall is to:

A. year   B. autumn   C. leaf   D. season   E. winter

Christmas is to December as Thanksgiving is to:

A. Month   B. date   C. celebrate   D. November

Chapter 8
Abbreviations

I have the student pick an abbreviation for the classmates to try to figure out. I introduce the abbreviation and then allow them to take time to discuss it. If they seem to have trouble, I start by giving them hints like what category it is in, such as months, streets, days of the week, title or is it an acronym. There are so many abbreviations that you will have no problem using one a day and not repeating an abbreviation during the year. It may surprise you just how many of the students do not know abbreviations and that is why I have incorporated it during calendar.

A website that I use for this is www.factmonster.com. Select the 'Wordwise' icon, then the 'Speaking of Language', and then scroll down to 'Common Abbreviations'.

Chapter 9
What Would You Do?

This promotes discussion among the students during calendar. I present a situation everyday for the topic and students discuss the best solution. This can range from safety at home to bullying at school. The children learn, over the course of the year, that their answer to almost every situation is to notify an adult that they trust, either a teacher or a parent. Our children are subject to many more dangerous situations than a generation ago and to role play and discuss scenarios help them to practice the right strategy. There are many websites for this and many situations I come up with, especially when a student comes and tells me about something that happened to them.

An example might be...

> You're CD shopping with a friend. While you're in one aisle and he's in another, you see him drop a CD into his backpack. What Would You Do?

or

> A good friend is struggling to keep up in math class. During a test, he whispers for you to show him your answers. What Would You Do?

Chapter 10
Math Moment

This topic is usually in every calendar in every classroom. I find if something is working, then I should do it too. However, using the gaming approach, the student earns play money if the answer is correct. If he has to have a friend help him with the problem of the day, then he has to split the money with the friend. They love the challenge of trying to do it themselves and the students in the room are excited when they know the answer and each one wants to help him. We discuss the process of how to work the problem. I like to use holiday themed problems when appropriate. It keeps the Math Moment fresh. Sometime during the year, I post a menu and we take two weeks discussing different scenarios to each student that they have to figure out how much their bill would be if they ordered different things and what their change should be. This helps to show the practical reason why they have to learn math. I also take sometime during the year to introduce an actual checkbook, deposit slips and withdrawal forms from our local bank and they practice using them. They learn the correct way to write out a check and how to keep the register accurate by subtracting their check from the total to see what is left in the checking account. They love this process. Some days, I don't use paper at all. I'll go to the board and tell them that I am thinking of a number that is for example less than 300 but more than 100. They take turns trying to figure out the number and I encourage them to use the less than, more than terminology. This makes the whole classroom engaged in this activity. There are many Math Moments that you can produce. Keep it fresh and help them be ready for the standardized testing. There are handy math quizzes in the back of the Every

Day Counts Calendar Math by Gillespie-Kanter book. I use these questions when I allow the students to pick a Math Problem for the day.

Chapter 11
Mystery State

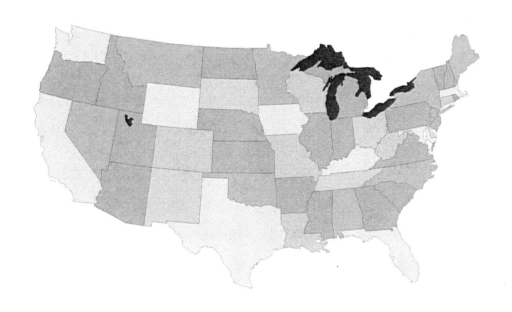

This is one of the student's favorites. They have the opportunity to make big money. I use the website www.educationworld.com. Place the pointer on 'Top Features' and select 'Worksheet Library', scroll down the page and select 'Mystery States' and print off their worksheets. Each state is presented with five facts. I start with number one and read the fact and tell them that if they guess the state, they can earn $500 play money. Usually the fact is little known but sometimes the students will surprise you by knowing the first one presented. The second question is worth $400, the third is worth $300, the fourth $200 and finally they usually guess it on fifth question and receive $100, however, they have learned some facts that they didn't know about the state in the process. I also give them two bonus questions. The first is to tell me the abbreviation for the state and the second is to name the state capital. Each of the bonus questions are worth an extra hundred dollars each.

Chapter 12
Georgia

It is wonderful to have the opportunity to teach the children during Calendar something that their home state has to offer. Its rich history and endless venues make this part of calendar an easy way to present about where they live. I also present this segment as a multiple choice question and let them earn play money. If they have to call on another student to help them, then they have to split the winnings. There are many websites that I use and sometimes I can get ideas from their textbooks. Some websites are:

www.funtrivia.com Scroll to the bottom of the page and enter 'Georgia' in the 'Search Trivia Database'.

www.factmonster.com Select the 'United States' icon, then 'Profiles of Each State' under 'The Fifty States' section, choose the state you wish to inquire on.

Examples of Questions might be…

What is the state flower of Georgia?
A. Indian Paintbrush   B. Moccasin Flower
C. Black-eyed Susan   D. Cherokee Rose

Which of these great inventions was developed in Georgia?
A. Steamboat   B. Telegraph   C. Cotton Gin   D. wireless radio

Where can guests see how a real news television station works?
A. Piedmont Park   B. Inside CNN Studio Tour
C. The Laughing Skull Lounge   D. High Museum of Art

A tiny pest decimated Georgia's cotton economy during the Great Depression of the 1930's. What was this pest?
A. The Boll Weevil   B. The Cotton Termite
C. The Colorado Beetle   D. Terminus Maximus

The Cherokee people that once inhabited the region of Georgia, were removed to the Oklahoma territory beginning in 1832, with the distribution of Cherokee lands among white prospectors. What was the name given to the long march in which thousands died?

A. The Trail of Tears   B. The western Trail   C. The Long Trail
D. The OklahomaTrail

Chapter 13
Idiom

In A Pickle!

Many students take things literally. We introduce an Idiom each day and discuss the meaning. I tell them that if I hear them using the idiom throughout the course of the day in conversation that they could earn $100 play money. An example might be to "Not let the cat out of the bag". We would discuss how this does not mean that there is actually a cat in a bag and we need to let it out but, however that you should not expose a secret. I give them an opportunity to guess what the idiom means before I let the cat out of the bag! There are so many idioms that you will not have a problem introducing a different one each day for the whole year.

Some websites that I use are:

www.idiomconnection.com Select 'Arm, Hand, & Finger Idioms'.

www.eslhq.com Select the 'Worksheet' tab and search for 'Idioms'.

Chapter 14
Blurt®

For this topic, I actually use the cards out of the board game Blurt®. These questions have a wide range of subjects which I find useful to create a well rounded calendar. Most of the questions are pretty easy which makes the student feel successful. Of course, they can earn $100 for a correct answer; however, I challenge them by giving them the choice to earn $200 for a harder question. These I get off the question flash cards that correspond with the appropriate grade. They find these really challenging. I allow them to choose a friend to help them; however they have to split the money. Some examples of Blurt® questions are:

A building made of glass in which plants are grown – greenhouse

A written history of someone's life – biography

A bunch of flowers – bouquet

A woman who is the ruler of a kingdom - Queen

Chapter 15
Fact Monster

®

This is played like a game. Each student has the option not to participate but if they participate they must follows the rules. I read a Fact Monster question and if they get it right, they win monopoly money, however, if they get it wrong, they have to pay me money. The website that I find the questions is www.factmonster.com.

Some examples are...

Which of the inventions below was not invented by Thomas Edison?

    A. light bulbs   B. phonograph   C. telephone

Are reptiles cold-blooded or warm-blooded?

    A. cold-blooded   B. warm-blooded

The outermost color of the rainbow is red. What is a rainbow's innermost color?

    A. green   B. yellow   C. violet

Some baseball players are "southpaws" what is a "southpaw"?

    A. a pitcher who sometimes pitches underhand

    B. a pitcher who throws with his left hand

    C. a pitcher who grew up in the southern United States

Chapter 16
Amazing Fact

The Amazing Facts Section of the Calendar is mostly done for fun. It gives the students a chance to think and if they doubt the fact presented, it allows them to research it later and present their findings to the class the next day. There is no money for this section because there is no right or wrong answer. I allow the students to reach in the bag and select a fact to read to the group. There are so many websites for this but my fifth grade students love the most unusual and grossest facts that I can come up with.

Here are some websites:

www.stephencarr.com/facts.html

www.tealdragon.net/humor Select 'Facts' from the left hand column.

Some samples of these amazing facts might be:

1. A snail can sleep for three years.

2. Recycling one glass jar saves enough energy to watch T.V. for three hours.

3. No word in the English language rhymes with month, orange, silver and purple.

4. Honeybees have hair on their eyes.

5. Slugs have four noses.

6. Cockroaches are so hardy that they can even live nine days without their heads before they starve to death.

7. Women fart three times more often than men.

8. Toilet paper was invented in 1857.

9. There are seven points on the Statue of Liberty's crown.

Chapter 17

What Am I?

I use this section to help reinforce Language Arts. We cover many categories throughout the year. The students pick a problem out of a bag and try to solve it. I introduce prefixes, suffixes, antonyms, synonyms, noun, pronouns, verbs, adverbs, adjectives, root words, compound words, homophones, and contractions. I reward the students with play money which they can spend on Fridays.

Many of these questions come from the following websites:

www.superteacherworksheets.com Select topics in the 'ELA – Language Arts' section.

www.All-About-Spelling.com

Some examples of questions might be…

We usually have to be in bed at_____ (ate, eight)

What is the synonym for friendly?

The popular kids are very well liked by many. What are the synonyms?

Left is to right as down is to _____?

What two words make up the contraction; can't?

Name a compound word.

What is the verb in this sentence? The boy ran home.

Circle the noun in this sentence. California is a great place to live.

I also use a chart for one of the months to help the students learn about their address. It has the following titles:

My name is	Street Address
Zip Code	City
County	State
Region	Country
Continent	Hemisphere

Chapter 18
Joke Of The Day

I use this section to help develop their sense of humor. Of course, being fifth graders they like me to find the grossest jokes that I can. Some of my jokes of the day and cartoon articles which gives them a variety. I use knock-knock jokes, picture jokes, what am I riddles, seasonal jokes, and as many kinds that I can find. Sometimes, I like to find jokes relating to the topic that we are studying such as space, weather, etc.

Here are some websites that I use.

www.ducksters.com/jokes for kids

www.brownielocks.com

www.e-teacher-discounts.com Scroll down and select 'Jokes'

Some examples of these are:

How much do pirates pay for their earrings?
Buccaneer

What did the camel wear when he went into the jungle to hunt?
Camelflage

What is alligator's favorite drink?
Gatorade

Why did the kid cross the park?
To get to the other slide!

What goes "ha, ha, plop"?
Someone laughing their head off.

Knock Knock!
Who's there?
Little old Lady.
Little old lady who?
I didn't know you could yodel!

Chapter 19
Manners

Many students have never been taught the most basic manners.

We begin the year talking about the manners and rules that have been set up in the cafeteria.

We proceed to talking about manners in the everyday classroom which involve, raising your hand, waiting your turn, and standing in line and especially how to make new friends and be a friend. In our school we have many 'special needs' students so we talk about manners when we see them which may include being friendly, don't point, don't talk about them and especially don't laugh at them.

For the month of November, we talk about table manners, introducing a new table manner everyday. If I see the student exercising this new manner in the lunch room that day, they are rewarded with a hundred dollars of play money which they could spend on Friday at Trading Post.

I like to introduce the correct way to answer the telephone and what to do at a Birthday Party. What do you do if you receive a present that you already have or that you really didn't like?

There are so many manners to learn that I have no problem teaching one a day for the entire school year.

Simple examples are:

It's okay to laugh if someone trips or burps.
    True or False

It is not polite to whisper in front of other people
    True or False

Your Aunty sends you a music voucher for your birthday, what do you do?
    A. Go out and spend it, and play the CD extra loud next time she comes around
    B. Write her a letter or phone her to thank her

C. Forget she even sent it to you and find it six months later under all your magazines.

At dinner, when should you start eating?
   A. As soon as you are served. B. When everyone has been served.
   C. When the host or parent begins to eat.

Some websites that I like to use are…

www.childdevelopmentinfo.com Place the cursor on the 'Parenting' tab, then on 'Socialization' then select 'Manners'.

www.familyeducation.com Search for 'Manners' then select 'Manners for Kids (and Parents)'.

Chapter 20
$100 Question

Our $100 question is only given on Friday as an extra chance to earn a hundred dollars for the Trading Post. This is a chance for me to present the typical calendar questions.

A website for this is www.enchantedlearning.com

Some examples of questions might be:

Which word is spelled correctly?
    A. Wendesday
    B. Wensday
    C. Wednesday

Determine if the sentence is fact or opinion

    School begans in August.

    How many months are two years?

    What is the first month of every year?

    Summer comes right after_____.

    12:01 AM is just after _____.Midnight or noon

    Every four years there is a _____ that has an extra day.

Chapter 21
Famous Person in History

This is one of the most favorite topics for the students to do. I read a little bit about the product, and they have to guess what it is or I tell them about the product, and they have to guess the inventor. It's a fun game and it sharpens their listening skills as well as processing the information for an answer that makes sense. You could incorporate famous Politicians, Authors, World Leaders, Athletes, Musicians and Current Events. There is enough information on the internet, a new topic can be introduced every day for the whole year.

An example of this might be:

"Josephine married a man who worked for a company that manufactured gauze and adhesive tape called Johnson & Johnson. We will never know the reason, but it is a fact that Josephine was accident prone. During the first week that she was married to Earle Dickson, she cut herself twice with the kitchen knife. After that, it just went from bad to worse. It seemed that Josephine was always cutting herself. One day her husband had an idea. He sat down with some tape and gauze and a pair of scissors. Then he cut the tape into strips. In the middle of each strip he stuck a little square of gauze."

The BAND-AID was adopted.

Chapter 22
Where's
Mrs. Vonderspeilen?

This sweet Lady travels to different and interesting places around the world each day. I have a tapestry bag that Mrs. Vonderspeilen keeps her beautiful hat in. She puts on her hat, lowers her glasses, and immediately develops an accent which the children adore. She reads the most fascinating facts about where she is visiting, holds up a picture, and challenges the students to try to guess where she is. They love the performance and all the fun Mrs. Vonderspeilen has. She is a character that all the children admire. Even though there is no money reward for this segment of the calendar, the children can't wait until Mrs. Vonderspeilen shows up. Her travels can be researched on the internet so that you have another exciting place to visit every day. Why doesn't Mrs. Vonderspeilen come visit your classroom today?

An example might be:

"Last week I had another exciting adventure! This very unusual city is called the "City of Water." Can you believe everybody gets around by boat because there aren't any cars here? This city has 150 canals and 400 bridges and it includes more than 100 islands! I took a ride in one of the long black boats called a gondola. The gondolier is the person who gave me the boat ride. He wore a straw hat with a long black ribbon on it and a traditional striped shirt. To steer the boat through the narrow canals, he used long poles.

Can you guess where I visited?

Venice in Italy

Chapter 23
Stump The Teacher

This section gives a student the opportunity to become the teacher. There are two ways of doing this. One way, is to ask the Calendar Helper to research some information and have a question ready in the morning. They can get their information from the internet or from a book but they must have written proof of their answer. However, sometimes students forget to be prepared so then we play Stump the teacher a different way. The students' write down a word as proof of the answer and then the teacher has the opportunity to ask up to 10 questions that require yes or no answers, to reveal the right answer. If the teacher gets stumped, the students get to choose one piece of candy to eat at their snack time. Teachers, this is a good exercise to help you stay sharp. The students love being the winners and they are winners in the classroom because they have worked as a team to Stump The Teacher!

Chapter 24
Where Am I?

This develops the students map reading skills. I introduce a different kind of map where the students have to not only be able to read the map but answer a question for play money. We introduce a physical map, political map and reading maps on a grid. We especially like to review latitude and longitude, and hemispheres. Some other maps we touch upon are rainfall and temperature maps, land use maps, population maps and learn about time zones. We also learn about different regions in the United States and how a map is different that a globe. There are so many maps that you could introduce a new style each month of the year and challenge them with questions on how locate destinations. They sharpen their skill of reading the Legend and using a Map Scale. These will be important life skills that they will need to have. Of course, the right answers are rewarded with play money, but the real benefit is to use this skill later in everyday life.

Chapter 25
Word Of The Day

The students have fun with this. You can get your words off the internet, from your lesson plans or even from a dictionary. We introduce a new word each day, explain what kind of word it is and its definition. We then put it into a sentence and challenge the students. If I hear the word used properly throughout the day, then they receive the play money that we have established as incentive. They can spend the money on Friday at the Trading Post. This increases their vocabulary and introduces new ways to say the same thing. By the end of the year, out students have increased their vocabulary by at least 180 new words and so have I!

Chapter 26
Index Card Topics

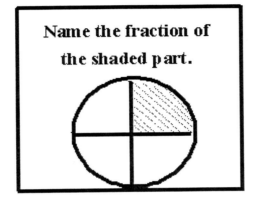

Name the fraction of
the shaded part.

I have many ideas for the Calendar that might help increase reinforcing topics taught throughout the year. My calendar is set up with one half of a small index card in each calendar pocket slot positioned so the student cannot read it ahead of time. This promotes the element of surprise and letting the student get used to answering a question without being prepared. I change the topic each month to let them practice on things that they may be weak in. Of course, the calendar helper is rewarded with play money each day for a correct answer.

Some examples are:

August – Grab Bag (I give clues to what word I am trying to have them guess)

September – Patterns (What comes next in the pattern)

October – Riddles (guess the answer to the riddle)

November – Table Manners (We review proper table manners and practice them at lunchtime)

December – Wants and Needs (We decide if the word on the card for the day is a want or a need)

January – Shapes (These are taken right out of our textbooks for age appropriate algebra terms)

February – Antonyms, Synonyms, and Homophone, (Student decided which one it is and talk about it)

March – Fact or Opinion? (Students decide if the statement on the card is a fact or not)

April – Estimation (This is a hard skill for students and this allows some extra Math practice)

May – Brain Teasers (This is the month that each student really gets challenged by solving puzzles)

Glossary

Trading Post - A table set up with bins filled with items students can purchase. The bins range from one to five "classroom bucks". The items can be donations of items or items purchased and range from school supplies, to tee shirts, and toys. This is quite the incentive the students need to be successful all week to earn the "classroom bucks".

Emotional Behavior Disorder (EBD) - In order for a student to be identified as EBD there are several key concepts to be addressed: (1) the student exhibits social, emotional or behavioral functioning that so departs from generally accepted, age appropriate ethnic or cultural norms that it adversely affects a child's academic progress, social relationships, personal adjustment, classroom adjustment, self-care or vocational skills; (2) the behaviors are severe, chronic, and frequent, occur at school and at least 1 other setting, and the student exhibits at least 1 of 8 characteristics or patterns of behavior indicative of EBD.

Criterion Referenced Competency Test (CRCT)   A test administered to students in the Georgia school system. Georgia's CRCT are used to determine how students are learning and performing in the Georgia school environment. Georgia law requires all third to eighth grade students to take the CRCT in the subjects of reading, language arts, and mathematics. Third to eighth graders also test in science and social studies.

Topic Container – I use pencil pouches fastened together but anything can be used.

Extreme Calendar Bulletin Board Examples

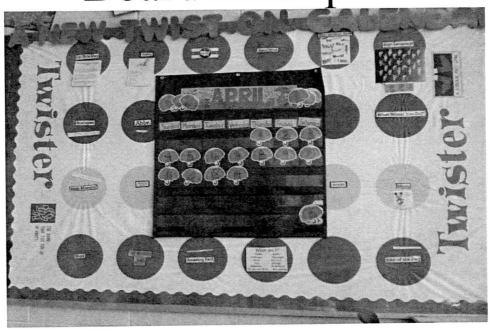

Acknowledgements

I wish to thank the following individuals and websites for allowing me to reference their material which has been a great asset for Extreme Calendar.

Kenn Nesbitt
  Poetry4Kids

Terry
  Fun Trivia™

Iram
  CanTeach

Bob Lisenko
  RHL School

Ken
  The Idiom Connection

Stephen Carr
  Teachers Index

Tim Weibel
  Super Teacher Worksheets

Ken
  Ducksters, Duck Software

Sam
  e-teacher-discounts

Mitchell Spector
  Enchanted Learning

Maria Gonzalez
  Educational Insights®
  Blurt®

Jim Loy

Linda and Marc
  Nursery Rhymes

Tracy Trimpe
  The Science Spot

Stephen Box
  Teach-Nology™

Mitchell Spector
  Enchanted Learning

Eric
  eslHQ

Scott & Stacy
  TealDragon

Merry
  All-About-Spelling

Sheila
  BrownieLocks

Robert Myers, PhD
  Child Development Institute

Terry
  Trivia Library

Jennie
  Family Education Network
  TeacherVision
  Enchanted Learning
  Fact Monster®